The Little Book of Look and Listen

Ideas for activities for the Foundation Stage

by Su Wall

Illustrations by Marion Lindsay

LITTLE BOOKS WITH BIG IDEAS

Published 2009 by A&C Black Publishers Limited
36 Soho Square, London W1D 3QY
www.acblack.com

ISBN 978-1-4081-1429-2

Text © Su Wall, 2009
Illustrations © Marion Lindsay 2009
Cover photographs © Shutterstock, 2009

Printed in Great Britain by Latimer Trend & Company Limited

This book is produced using paper that is made from wood grown in
managed, sustainable forests. It is natural, renewable and recyclable.

The logging and manufacturing processes conform to the environmental
regulations of the country of origin.

**To see our full range of titles
visit www.acblack.com**

Contents

Introduction

Welcome to The Little Book of Look and Listen. The book offers practitioners simple, yet effective activities to do with children – promoting listening and attention skills.

Little preparation is needed for most of the activities but plenty of imagination and making the best use of your environment will enhance any of these activities.

The activities have been designed using popular resources and equipment, which are found in most settings or can be easily collected or bought cheaply.

You do not need to do the activities in the order that they appear in this book – you can choose any activity from any page, or even integrate one activity with another to suit you and your children.

With each activity you will find the following features:

▶ Focus of the activity

▶ What you need

▶ Key words

▶ What to do

▶ Look, listen and note

▶ Taking the activity further (Taking it further)

In line with the Early Years Foundation Stage, practitioners must plan for the needs of all children, planning for their individual care and learning requirements.

The activities within this book can easily be adapted to meet the requirements of children with additional needs and can either be used on a one to one basis or in small groups.

The Environment

When planning any activity, it is key to think about the environment and how the environment will work best.

The Early Years Foundation Stage states 'The environment plays a key role in supporting and extending children's development and learning'.

How to promote an effective environment:

▶ Keep disruptions to a minimum

▶ Remove chairs away from tables, children will find it easier to reach and explore the activity

▶ Keep the surrounding environment quiet

▶ Remove TVs and radios

▶ Get down to the children's level and see how the environment looks from a child's perspective

Outdoor play is a requirement of the Early Years Foundation Stage and some children learn best when playing outside and are much happier outside. There are many natural resources that are readily available outside that can be used to promote many skills, especially listening skills, for children. Where possible, take the activity outside and observe the different responses you will get from the children and the activity.

Working in Partnership with Parents

In line with the Early Years Foundation Stage, it is vital to work in partnership with parents and carers.

Parents and families need to be valued as individuals. Trustworthy relationships need to be formed to be able to offer support with their child's development and learning.

During the activities within this book, take photographs, keep examples of children's work and display them for parents to see the progression their child is making.

Where possible, lend parents equipment and resources for them to enjoy at home with their child.

Top Tips for Successful Activities

▶ Work with your key children so you fully understand their interests and their development and learning.

▶ Observe and reflect the children's progress, where they are at developmentally, and plan the next steps accordingly.

▶ Listen to children, be patient and give them plenty of time to talk and respond.

▶ Don't interrupt a child when they are talking.

▶ Lead by example and use good spoken language.

▶ Work in small groups.

▶ Allow plenty of time for children to enjoy and complete the activities; try to go at the children's pace.

▶ Think about when is the best time for children to do the activity, ensuring they enjoy and benefit from the timing.

▶ Have realistic expectations for the children and activities that can be achieved.

▶ Join in with the activity and have fun with the children.

Development and Learning for Children

Children need to learn to listen and listening skills are key to any child's development and learning. Alongside speaking, listening skills will build the foundations for literacy.

An attention span is the ability to focus and sustain interest on an object, an activity, or a resource. It is the practitioner's role to provide suitable activities during the day that will engage and keep the child interested.

Early Years Foundation Stage: Developmental Matters

The activities within this book link to the following Early Learning Goals

Personal, Social, Emotional Development:

▶ Maintain attention, concentrate and sit quietly when appropriate

Communication, Language and Literacy

▶ Interact with others, negotiating plans and activities, taking turns in conversation

▶ Enjoy listening to and using spoken and written language, and readily turn to it in their play and learning

▶ Sustain attentive listening, responding to what they have heard with relevant comments, questions or actions

▶ Listen with enjoyment, and respond to stories, songs and other music, rhymes and poems and make up their own stories, songs, rhymes and poems

▶ Speak clearly and audibly with confidence and control and show awareness of the listener

Spot the Difference

Focus

Concentrating whilst identifying the differences

What you need:

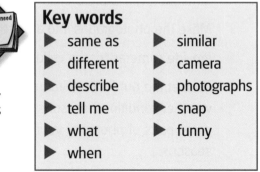

- digital camera
- laminator
- a variety of props
  including hats, glasses, gloves,
  wigs, bags, buckets and shoes

Key words

- same as
- different
- describe
- tell me
- what
- when
- similar
- camera
- photographs
- snap
- funny

What to do:

1. Take two pictures of each child, one photograph slightly different to the other one, e.g. one picture with the child wearing a hat, one without a hat. Let them choose how to make themselves look different

2. Print out the pictures and laminate. (If you do not have a laminator, you could cover the photos with clear plastic.)

3. Show the pictures to the children and see if they can spot the differences between the two pictures of each child.

4. Discuss the differences and see if they can match each other's pictures.

5. Use the pictures in various games such as Snap, Pairs or Spot the Difference.

Look, listen and note:

▶ Matching and sorting

▶ Listening, understanding and following instructions

▶ Working together

Taking it further

▶ When taking the photographs, have more than one difference for the children to notice on each picture or very slight differences between the photographs. This could be as simple as different facial expressions.

▶ Make the photographs into a matching game or dominoes.

▶ Provide cameras for the children to use to take their own pictures.

▶ Look at the outdoor environment and how it changes in different weather conditions, seasons and at different times of day. Take some pairs of photos of your garden in different weathers and seasons.

My Granny's Washing Line

Focus
Working together

What you need:

- pegs
- a washing line
- a variety of different items of either children's clothes or dolls' clothes
- different sized washing baskets or buckets
- 'washing powder' and 'fabric conditioner' bottles made out of labelled empty plastic bottles filled with soapy water
- paper and pens
- a water tray
- waterproof overalls

Key words

- clean
- dirty
- washing
- wash
- washing powder
- hot
- cold
- pegs

- wet
- dry
- windy
- sunny
- pairs
- matching
- sorting
- folding

Safety notice
Do not use real washing powder and detergent as some children may be allergic to the chemicals in these. Use soapy water.

What to do:

1. In the water tray place a variety of clothes for the children to wash.

2. Next to the water tray have a trolley filled with the baskets, pegs, washing powder and fabric conditioner. (A table can be used instead of a trolley.)

3. Let the children wash the clothes together, using warm and cold water.

4. Now help them to put their wet washing into a basket and take outside.

5. Peg the washing onto the washing line, helping each other and taking turns.

6. When washing is dry, match and sort the clothes into colours, sizes and types of clothes.

Look, listen and note:

▶ Working together – sharing, taking turns, copying and watching

▶ Listening to one another

▶ Fun and enjoyment

Taking it further

▶ The washing line can become a number line by numbering the pegs.

▶ Fold and sort the clothes.

▶ Discuss the wet and dry process of washing.

▶ Role-play washing the clothes at a laundrette, using cardboard boxes as washing machines and driers.

▶ Visit a laundrette within the local community.

▶ Discuss various methods of washing clothes – including how we used to wash clothes and how washing is washed differently in other parts of the world.

▶ Talk about different clothes for different times – seasonal, cultural, walking, exercise, weddings, etc.

Sound Lotto

Focus

A listening game

What you need:

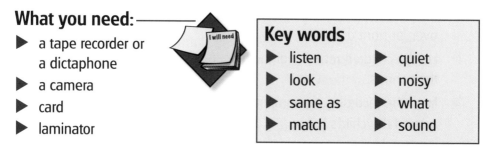

- a tape recorder or a dictaphone
- a camera
- card
- laminator

I will need

Key words

- listen
- look
- same as
- match
- quiet
- noisy
- what
- sound

What to do:

1. Go round the environment and record familiar sounds such as a kettle, washing machine, doors opening and closing, door bell, keys or hoover.

2. Take photographs of each object that you have recorded the sound of. Or find and cut out photos of them from magazines or catalogues.

3. Print, laminate and make the photographs into a lotto game. You need a baseboard for each player with four or six photos. Each board needs at least one picture that is on no other card. Then, make some single photo cards that are the same as the photos on the baseboards. Spread these cards out, face up on the carpet. Now play the sound recording, stopping after the first sound. The first child to spot the object on their baseboard calls out the name and can cover the picture on their baseboard with the matching single photo card.

4. Continue until all pictures on the baseboards have been covered.

5. In a quiet area, play the sounds, can the children match the sounds to the pictures?

6. Talk about each sound in detail – what it sounds like, what it's used for.

Look, listen and note:

▶ listening and identifying sounds
▶ listening, understanding and responding to instructions
▶ working together – sharing, turn taking

Taking it further

▶ Record sounds outside.

▶ Record similar sounds e.g. which door is opening – the fridge, the oven or front door?

▶ Let the children record their own sounds – their voices, sounds of their shoes.

▶ Lend the recording equipment to parents to record sounds from around the child's home.

What's That?

Focus

Listening to a variety of sounds; Identifying and recognising the difference between sounds

What you need:

- a quiet area
- a large box with a lid
- a variety of objects – some that make a noise when shaken and some that don't (e.g. keys, coins, saucepans, rattle, cup and teaspoons, plastic bottle with stones in, crinkly paper and pebbles)

I will need

Key words

- listen to
- look
- sounds like
- quiet
- noisy
- same as
- different
- predict
- rattle
- crash
- bang
- slowly
- quickly
- fast
- hard

What to do:

1. Sit with the children, a smaller group is preferable, in the quiet area and talk to the children about the various objects you have collected from the environment.

2. Using one item at a time, show the children the sound each object makes when it is shaken.

3. Without the children seeing it, put one object in the box and ask a child to shake the box gently and guess what is inside

4. Involve the other children by asking them if the child identified the noise correctly.

Look, listen and note:

▶ Listening to instructions

▶ Matching and sorting sounds

▶ Working together

▶ Showing curiosity and imagination

Taking it further

▶ Shake the objects either quietly or noisily, quickly or slowly to offer a range of various sounds just from one object.

▶ Talk about the objects, what would we do with them, where have we found them, where are they kept, have you got any at home, are there any similarities between objects?

▶ Tell the children to close their eyes and listen carefully to the sounds.

▶ Use a variety of musical instruments.

▶ Take the children outside and listen to the sounds – aeroplanes, birds, trees, wind chimes,

▶ Go out in the local community and record familiar sounds.

Do This!

Focus
Taking turns, copying and following instructions

What you need:
- a large open space indoors or outdoors

I will need

Key words
- copy me
- follow
- do this
- repeat
- watch
- listen
- sequence
- imitate

What to do:

1. Help the children to stand in a circle all facing inwards holding hands.

2. Now ask the children to copy you by holding one hand up in the air or stand on one leg or jump about.

3. Praise the children for their efforts.

4. Now choose a child to be the next leader. You may need to give them some ideas such as clapping hands, walking backwards or hopping.

5. Encourage all the children to have a turn at being the leader. Join in yourself and follow the leader.

Look, listen and note:

▶ Listening and responding

▶ Listens to peers

▶ Interacts with others

Taking it further

▶ Use a range of resources to aid the game – balls and beanbags.

▶ Number the children – take it in turns to be leader.

▶ Take the game all around the environment.

▶ Play Simon Says.

▶ Use different tempos to alter the speed of your actions for example, very slow, very quick movements.

Surprise!

Focus

Guess and imagine what's in the surprise box!

What you need:

- an empty box with a lid such as a shoe box
- wrapping paper
- a range of objects – bunch of keys, a book, a letter, a torch, a hat, a game.

I will need

Key words

- surprise
- look
- imagine
- speak
- listen
- shake
- wrapped
- noisy
- quiet
- inside
- outside
- guess

What to do:

1. Put a range of interesting objects into the box and wrap the box up in wrapping paper.

2. When the children are not around place the box outside where it will be easily found.

3. When the children 'find' the box, talk about whose box is it, where did it come from?

4. Guess what's in the box. Shake it, listen to sounds, pick the box up – is it heavy/light?

5. Allow time for children to speculate what's in the box.

6. Open the box carefully, using an expressive tone of voice to maintain the interest and curiosity.

7. Look inside and enjoy exploring what's in the box.

Look, listen and note:

▶ Shows curiosity and anticipation

▶ Explores and uses imagination

▶ Joins in activities

▶ Attention span – how long did they stay engaged?

Taking it further

▶ Hide the box – in a bush, under a table.

▶ Theme the box – all one colour, seasonal objects, fruit and vegetables, dressing up clothes.

▶ Allow a child to open the box.

▶ Make a prop box for a favourite story.

▶ Have more that one box, compare what's in the box – What's the same? What's different?

▶ Children can make their own box for other children to explore.

Against the Clock

Focus

Using timers to focus children's attention whilst playing a memory game

What you need:

- a tray
- a tea towel
- a timer (the wind-up 'pinger' sort is good for these games)
- a range of 8 or less objects – keys, pencil, toy, hair accessory, ring, letter, piece of fruit, book, etc.

I will need

Key words

- look
- remember
- see
- hear
- tray
- time
- spot
- same as
- gone
- missing
- quick
- ready
- steady
- go

What to do:

1. Sit in a circle with the children.

2. Start with five items.

3. Introduce each object. Talk about what it is, what it's used for, pass it round for children to touch.

4. Place all the objects on the tray and cover with the tea towel.

5. Now ask the children to close their eyes while you take an object away.

6. Start the timer. Can the children remember the objects and tell what is missing before the timer runs out?

Look, listen and note:

▶ Listening and following instructions

▶ Memory and recall

▶ Attention span – how long did they stay engaged?

▶ Fun and enjoyment

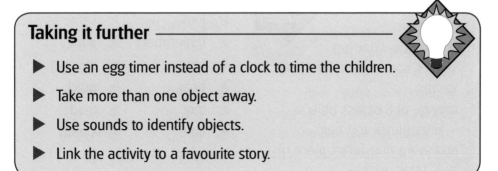

Taking it further

▶ Use an egg timer instead of a clock to time the children.

▶ Take more than one object away.

▶ Use sounds to identify objects.

▶ Link the activity to a favourite story.

Feel the Difference

Focus
Exploring textures

What you need:

▶ a number of shallow containers, such as plant trays

▶ a range of materials with different textures such as sand, soil, sawdust, flour, shredded paper, fabric, dried pasta or rice

Key words

▶ soft
▶ hard
▶ rough
▶ smooth
▶ natural
▶ different

▶ same as
▶ similar
▶ hot
▶ cold
▶ sticky

What to do:

1. Fill the containers with the range of textures and place on a table/ the floor.

2. Talk to the children about the textures and show them each one individually.

3. Let the children explore one texture at a time.

4. Discuss what it feels like, its' properties, what it's used for.

5. Wash your hands.

6. Repeat until all the textures have been explored.

7. Be aware of allergies!

Look, listen and note:

▶ Shows curiosity

▶ Explores and uses imagination

▶ Joins in activities

▶ Attention span – how long did they stay engaged?

Taking it further

▶ Discuss similarities between textures.

▶ Explore using feet as well as hands.

▶ Cover up the textures with fabrics, just explore using touch.

▶ Experiment with textures. What happens if you:

  ▷ Add hot or cold water – be careful when using hot water;

  ▷ Mix with another material;

  ▷ Add food colouring?

▶ Take the activity outside. Feel the difference with natural textures found in the garden – soil, leaves, bark, flowers, grass.

What's Next?

Focus
Sequencing their day

What you need:
- camera
- laminator (optional)
- box

I will need

Key words
- next
- follow on
- before
- after
- order
- sequence
- missing

What to do:

1. Take a range of photographs of your children's typical day, print and laminate them.

2. Place photographs into the box.

3. Sit the children with you in a circle and place the box on the floor.

4. Take out a photograph and talk through with the children what is happening in the photograph as part of their daily routine.

5. Pass each child a photograph and let them describe the picture.

6. Working together, sequence the photographs in the order of their typical day.

Look, listen and note:

▶ Describes what they can see

▶ Joins in activities, takes turns to participate

▶ Sequencing

Taking it further

▶ Take a couple of photographs out of the box. Can the children identify what's missing?

▶ Make the sequence of photographs into a book by using treasury tags to join photographs together.

▶ Put photographs in that don't belong e.g. a photograph of a cat! Can children identify that it doesn't fit the sequence?

▶ Use photographs with the children to tell a story.

▶ Buy disposable cameras and let children take their own photographs of their day at home/at your setting.

Take a Peek

Focus

The fun of dens

What you need:

- a large piece of fabric such as a parachute or a blanket and a table or other structure for your den
- a selection of empty boxes
- range of torches, binoculars and mirrors

I will need

Key words

- hide
- dark
- spook
- look
- peeps
- where
- gone
- blanket
- mirror
- shine
- explore
- torch
- binoculars
- box

What to do:

1. Help children to make a den, by draping the fabric over the table.

2. Put the range of torches, mirrors and binoculars in the boxes and hide them in the den.

3. Invite a small group of children to go into the den and explore the boxes, taking a peek in each box.

4. Using the fabric, play peek-a-boo with the children while they find the items. Be aware, some children may be frightened of the dark.

Look, listen and note:

▶ Explores and uses imagination

▶ Shows curiosity

▶ Interacts with others

▶ Fun and enjoyment

Taking it further

▶ Turn the lights out – use the torches to find each other in the den.

▶ Use the torches to make patterns, reflections.

▶ Make binoculars using different coloured cellophane.

▶ Play hide and seek outside.

▶ Act out 'We're going on a bear hunt'.

▶ Use a tent.

▶ Make animal dens – let's be lions!

Who's Next?

Focus
Looking, listening and paying attention

What you need:
- a large carpeted area
- ball

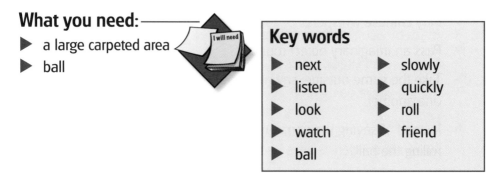

Key words
- next
- listen
- look
- watch
- ball
- slowly
- quickly
- roll
- friend

What to do:

1. Sit in a circle with the children.

2. Say a child's name and gently roll the ball to that child.

3. The child chooses a friend, says their name and rolls the ball to them.

4. Continue until all the children have had a go.

Look, listen and note:

▶ Listens, understands and responds

▶ Working together, taking turns, sharing, copying

▶ Physical coordination

▶ Attention span – how long did they stay engaged?

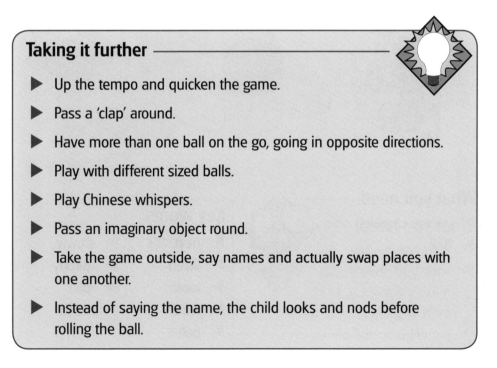

Taking it further

▶ Up the tempo and quicken the game.

▶ Pass a 'clap' around.

▶ Have more than one ball on the go, going in opposite directions.

▶ Play with different sized balls.

▶ Play Chinese whispers.

▶ Pass an imaginary object round.

▶ Take the game outside, say names and actually swap places with one another.

▶ Instead of saying the name, the child looks and nods before rolling the ball.

In the Bag

Focus
Listening skills

What you need:
- a drawstring bag
- variety of objects that make a noise e.g. keys, bells, cup and spoon, rattle
- a quiet carpeted area

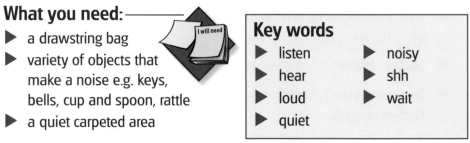

I will need

Key words
- listen
- hear
- loud
- quiet
- noisy
- shh
- wait

What to do:

1. Before the game, place all the objects in the bag and close the drawstring.

2. Sit with the children and introduce the bag.

3. Use an excited voice to gain the children's attention, 'What do you think you will be able to hear?'

4. Place all the items on a tray with the bag. Cover everything with a cloth and slide one or two objects into the bag under the cloth.

5. Shake each object. Can the children guess what is making the sound?

Look, listen and note:

▶ Matching and identifying sounds

▶ Listens and responds

▶ Describes what they have seen

▶ Joins in activities, takes turns to participate

Taking it further

▶ Use a range of sound levels, quiet to loud sounds.

▶ Increase the number of objects in the bag.

▶ Go outside, listen to sounds – trees moving, walking through mud or leaves, mobiles, aeroplanes, cars.

▶ Prop bag linked to story – 'We're going on a bear hunt'.

▶ Just shake the object once.

▶ Listen to sounds all around the environment – a tap running, doors opening/shutting.

▶ Let the children make their own sound bags.

▶ Group the objects together, such as all musical instruments or all kitchen utensils.

Ready, Steady, Go!

Focus
Use anticipation to hold attention

What you need:
- chalk
- a large open space outside

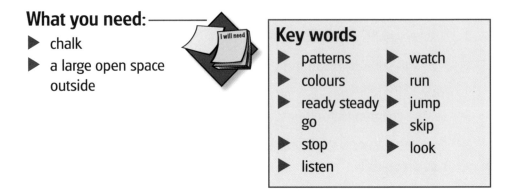

I will need

Key words
- patterns
- colours
- ready steady go
- stop
- listen
- watch
- run
- jump
- skip
- look

What to do:

1. Using the chalk, draw a line on the ground in a basic large pattern, such as a zigzag or a spiral.

2. Stand with the children at the beginning of the line and get ready to run following the pattern.

3. Say 'Ready, steady, go', taking the lead to show the children what to do.

4. Clap your hands and stop.

5. Repeat – using longer and shorter times and draw some different patterns to follow.

6. Vary the length between 'ready steady go' and 'stop'.

Look, listen and note:

▶ Listens, understands and responds to instructions

▶ Interacts with others

▶ Fun and enjoyment

Taking it further

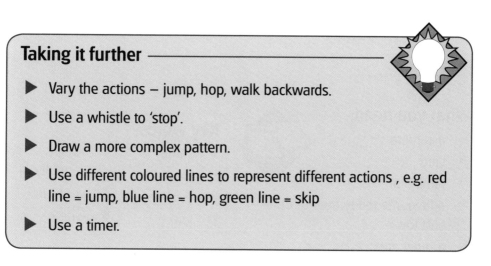

▶ Vary the actions – jump, hop, walk backwards.

▶ Use a whistle to 'stop'.

▶ Draw a more complex pattern.

▶ Use different coloured lines to represent different actions , e.g. red line = jump, blue line = hop, green line = skip

▶ Use a timer.

Together

Focus

Turn taking and memory skills playing picture pairs

What you need:

- a camera
- card
- laminator
- a favourite teddy bear or other soft toy
- a quiet area

I will need

Key words

- same
- two
- copy
- look
- watch carefully
- your turn
- where

What to do:

1. With the children go round the environment and take photos of the favourite teddy bear in different places such as 'teddy next to the flowers' and 'teddy reading a book'.

2. Take photos of at least 20 different situations.

3. Print out two copies of each picture and laminate, making cards.

4. Sit with the children and turn all the cards over face down.

5. In turn, let each child turn over two cards to try and find a pair. If incorrect turn the cards back over.

6. Continue the game until all the pairs have been found.

Look, listen and note:

▶ Listening and following instructions

▶ Memory and recall

▶ Attention span – how long did they stay engaged?

▶ Fun and enjoyment

Taking it further

▶ Go to your local community and take photographs of teddy at bus stops, the post office, park, bank etc.

▶ Increase the number of different situations.

▶ Increase the size of a photo and make a jigsaw.

▶ Instead of picture pairs, make a matching game.

▶ Let the children take their own photos.

▶ Let the children take teddy home and take photos in their own home environment.

1, 2, 3 Together

Focus

Stop, look, listen with a parachute

What you need:

- a large open space outside
- a parachute, preferably one with handles

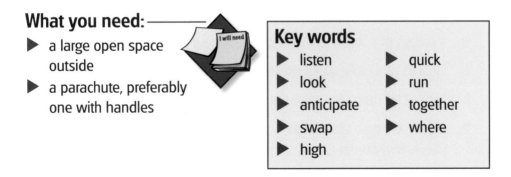

I will need

Key words

- listen
- look
- anticipate
- swap
- high
- quick
- run
- together
- where

What to do:

1. Stand in a circle with each child holding a handle of the parachute.

2. Carefully lift the parachute up and down. Repeat until the children are confident in using the parachute.

3. As you lift the parachute up, say two children's names, and let them swap places by running under the parachute before it comes down again.

4. Repeat until all the children have had a go!

Look, listen and note:

▶ Working and engaging with others

▶ Physical coordination

▶ Listens and responds to instructions

▶ Fun and enjoyment

Taking it further

▶ Swap places under the parachute in pairs.

▶ Children themselves choose who to swap with.

▶ Use a ball and try to bounce the ball on the parachute between two children

▶ Have favourite toys bouncing on the parachute – control and direct to a particular child.

Let's Grow

Focus
Attention and listening through dance

What you need:

- a large open, safe space
- 'The Tiny Seed' by Eric Carle
- 'Jasper's Beanstalk' by Mick Inkpen
- a selection of music (The Little Book of Dance track called 'Awakening' is a good one!)

I will need

Key words
- bulb
- seed
- plant
- grow
- soil
- wind
- water
- sun
- dance

- stretch
- sway
- move
- jiggle
- curl
- tiny
- tall
- each

What to do:

1. Read one of the stories with a group of children. Now introduce a dancing session on 'Let's Grow from a Seed'.

2. Provide enough space for each child to be able to dance and move freely whilst growing.

3. Movement/dance to include:

▷	bulb/seed	-	curl up into a tiny ball
▷	growth	-	slowly unroll and stretch and grow
		-	standing on tiptoes for full growth, hands open for petals
▷	wind	-	sway side to side in the wind
▷	watered	-	jiggle/shiver when being watered
▷	sun	-	dance around in the warmth.

Look, listen and note:

▶ Explores and uses imagination

▶ Physical coordination

▶ Listens and responds to instructions

▶ Fun and enjoyment

Taking it further

▶ Flowers wilt, so movement can return back down to a tiny ball.

▶ Make a thunderstorm – up the tempo and movement.

▶ Grow seeds with the children.

▶ Talk about life cycles – plants, caterpillars, frogs.

▶ Visit your local garden centre.

▶ Make up some cultural dances. (There are some ideas in The Little Book of Dance.)

Tracks and Mazes

Focus
Children's visual skills

What you need:

- a large table covered in paper, such as rolls of old wallpaper
- four colours of paint
- some lids, e.g. a plant saucer, a selection of wheeled toys e.g. cars, lorries
- a basket
- aprons

I will need

Key words
- tracks
- follow
- lines
- look
- colours
- find
- left
- right
- copy
- in front
- behind
- size of wheels
- patterns

What to do:

1. Cover the table in paper and put paint into the lids and wheeled toys into the basket.

2. Stand back and let the children create tracks and mazes using the wheeled toys dipped in paint.

3. Try giving some instructions: stop, go backwards, sideways, turn directions.

4. Use the wheeled toys to go between the tracks and mazes on an imaginary journey.

Look, listen and note:

▶ Enjoys own and others' mark making

▶ Sustains attentive listening

▶ Responds to instructions

▶ Has fun!

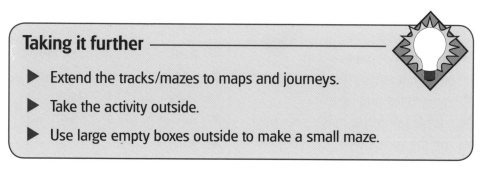

Taking it further

▶ Extend the tracks/mazes to maps and journeys.

▶ Take the activity outside.

▶ Use large empty boxes outside to make a small maze.

Let's Play

Focus
Attention skills through mark making

What you need:

- ▶ selection of mark making objects
- ▶ selection of paper – different sizes, colours, textures
- ▶ envelopes and labels
- ▶ used stamps (or make your own on the computer!)

Key words
- ▶ letters
- ▶ post
- ▶ writing
- ▶ copy
- ▶ follow
- ▶ write
- ▶ marks
- ▶ post person
- ▶ envelopes
- ▶ stamps
- ▶ size

What to do:

1. Set up a mark making area in a quiet corner of the room.

2. Put the selection of mark making objects into a basket and paper into another basket. A trolley would work too.

3. Move away from the area and just observe the children explore and use all the materials. When they are ready, you could introduce some of the extension activities, but make sure children always have opportunities to use the mark making area freely.

Look, listen and note:

▶ Explores and experiments with new textures and resources

▶ Enjoys own and others' mark making

▶ Engages with others

Taking it further

▶ Write letters with the children.

▶ Actually post letters to their home.

▶ Go to the Post Office and buy stamps.

▶ Read 'The Jolly Polly Postman'.

▶ Each day add another resource to the mark making area – post its, paperclips, hole-punch, treasury tags, used envelopes. Discuss what they are, how they got here, what they're used for.

Wet, Wet, Wet

Focus
Water wheels and dripping water

What you need: —
▶ water tray
▶ water wheels
▶ pipes
▶ watering cans
▶ empty plastic boxes and other containers

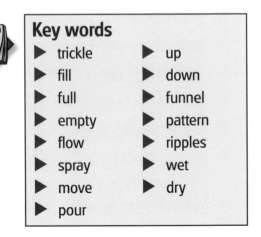

I will need

Key words
▶ trickle   ▶ up
▶ fill   ▶ down
▶ full   ▶ funnel
▶ empty   ▶ pattern
▶ flow   ▶ ripples
▶ spray   ▶ wet
▶ move   ▶ dry
▶ pour

What to do:

1. Fill the water tray up and make sure it is in a safe area with non-slip flooring.

2. Place all the resources in the water or on a trolley nearby.

3. Stay with the children as they explore and predict the joys of water – how water can move, patterns water makes, etc.

Look, listen and note:

▶ Shows curiosity, explores and experiments

▶ Working together, taking turns, sharing, copying

▶ Attention span – how long did they stay engaged?

Taking it further

▶ Introduce floating and sinking – boats, pebbles, sponges, shells.

▶ Add drops of food colouring into water – look at patterns, colours.

▶ Go outside – taking pipes, plastic guttering and water!

▶ Freeze coloured water.

▶ Group together objects in the water such as at the seaside – shells, boats, pebbles, sand.

▶ Add cornflour and watch what happens!

Where's the Treasure?

Focus
Sustaining attention

What you need:
- a water tray
- shredded paper and some shiny treasure – keys, jewellery, money

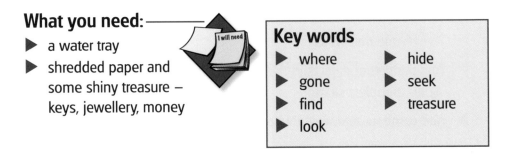

I will need

Key words
- where
- gone
- find
- look
- hide
- seek
- treasure

What to do:

1. Fill the water tray with shredded paper.

2. Sit with the children and show them the 'treasure'.

3. Go and hide the treasure in the water tray.

4. Let each child find one piece of treasure at a time.

5. Celebrate when the treasure is found.

Look, listen and note:

▶ Shows curiosity and anticipation

▶ Explores and uses imagination

▶ Joins in activities, takes turns to participate

▶ Attention span – how long did they stay engaged?

Taking it further

▶ Use magnetic treasure and use magnets to hunt the treasure.

▶ Play hide and seek outside.

▶ Hide 'treasure' outside and give children clues such as, 'You're getting warm', 'It's behind/in front of you'.

▶ Use a timer. Can the children find the treasure in time?

▶ Make treasure maps.

▶ Group the treasure – same colour or same sounds.

Find It

What you need:

▶ some photos of items of clothing (including hats, glasses, shoes) stuck on card to make picture cards

▶ a selection of clothes to match the photos

▶ a basket and mirrors

I will need

Key words
▶ copy	▶ disguise
▶ match	▶ hat
▶ same as	▶ glasses
▶ dress	▶ big
▶ look	▶ small
▶ mirror	

What to do:

1. Turn all the picture cards over.

2. In turn let the children turn a card over and talk about the item of clothing on the card.

3. Go and find the same item as on the card in the basket and put it on.

4. Look in the mirror and see what you are wearing.

5. Keep going and dress up in all sorts of clothing.

Look, listen and note:

▶ Selects and matches

▶ Working together, taking turns, copying and sharing

▶ Listens with enjoyment

▶ Explores and uses imagination

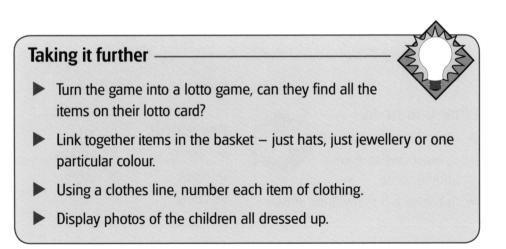

Taking it further

▶ Turn the game into a lotto game, can they find all the items on their lotto card?

▶ Link together items in the basket – just hats, just jewellery or one particular colour.

▶ Using a clothes line, number each item of clothing.

▶ Display photos of the children all dressed up.

Storytime

Focus
Listening skills

What you need:
- large floor cushions
- a quiet undisturbed area outside
- a basket full of favourite stories

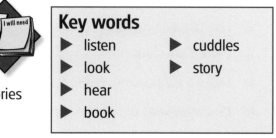

Key words
- listen
- look
- hear
- book
- cuddles
- story

What to do:

1. Make a story area outside by placing cushions in a shady and sheltered area – perhaps under a tree.

2. Sit with the children on the cushions and get comfy amongst each other.

3. Allow one child to pick a storybook from the basket and look at the book together.

4. Let each child choose a book to read together.

Look, listen and note:

▶ Listens with enjoyment to stories

▶ Retells stories

▶ Explores with imagination

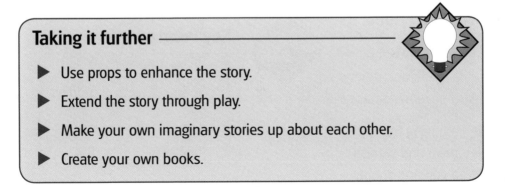

Taking it further

▶ Use props to enhance the story.

▶ Extend the story through play.

▶ Make your own imaginary stories up about each other.

▶ Create your own books.

Let's Bake

Focus
Attention skills

What you need:

- flour
- salt
- water
- bowls
- a baking tray
- paint and varnish
- a cup and spoon

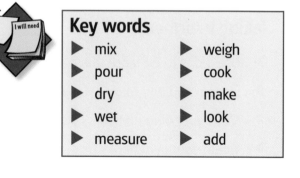

Key words

- mix
- pour
- dry
- wet
- measure
- weigh
- cook
- make
- look
- add

What to do:

1. Measure two cups of flour and mix with one cup of salt.

2. Help children to mix thoroughly and add enough water until the mixture becomes a stiff dough.

3. Share out the dough so each child has enough dough to create their own shape.

4. When the children are happy with their creations, you can bake them in an oven on a very low heat until hard.

5. Once cold, the children can paint them.

Look, listen and note:

▶ Listens, understands and responds to instructions

▶ Interacts with others

▶ Sustains their listening and attention throughout

▶ Fun and enjoyment

Taking it further

▶ Mix glitter into the mixture.

▶ Use scales to weigh out the ingredients.

▶ Make basic recipe cards for the children to follow.

▶ Instead of salt, use sand and let it dry naturally.

▶ Use clay to make hedgehogs, divas for Diwali or tree decorations for Christmas.

▶ Be creative. Make food for the home corner, animals for imaginary play.

▶ Give each child their own mixing bowl and ingredients to make their own dough.

▶ Make pastry – bake and eat!

Feel It

Focus

Look and watch

What you need:

- food colouring (blue and green)
- water
- a water tray
- various sizes of plastic containers that can be put in the freezer.
- a timer
- some small world arctic animals (seals, bears and penguins)
- camera
- dictaphone

I will need

Key words

- water
- freeze
- frozen
- melt
- blue
- cold
- ice
- icebergs

What to do:

1. Help the children to fill the containers with water and food colouring and freeze.

2. Once frozen, place the ice into the water tray with the arctic animals.

3. Allow the ice to start to melt, so it is safe to touch.

4. Create icebergs – watch what happens to the ice.

5. During the day, keep revisiting the water tray to look at and talk about what has happened, record it using a camera, dictaphone or drawings.

Look, listen and note:

▶ Explores and uses imagination

▶ Shows curiosity

▶ Interacts with others

▶ Fun and enjoyment

Taking it further

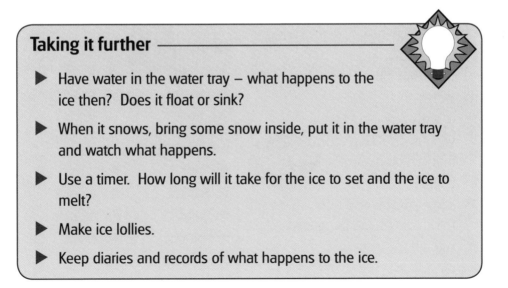

▶ Have water in the water tray – what happens to the ice then? Does it float or sink?

▶ When it snows, bring some snow inside, put it in the water tray and watch what happens.

▶ Use a timer. How long will it take for the ice to set and the ice to melt?

▶ Make ice lollies.

▶ Keep diaries and records of what happens to the ice.

Where Has It Gone?

Focus
Visual and listening skills

What you need:
▶ a soft toy
▶ a large area

Key words
▶ look
▶ where
▶ who
▶ behind
▶ in front

▶ pass
▶ quietly
▶ outside
▶ circle

What to do:

1. Stand the children closely in a circle with hands behind their backs.

2. Choose one child to stand in the middle and ask them to close their eyes while you give the soft toy to another child.

3. The soft toy is passed discreetly from one child to another until you say 'stop'.

4. The child in the middle has three guesses – who has got the soft toy?

5. When they have had three guesses, they choose another child for the middle. Stop when the children have had enough.

Look, listen and note:

▶ Listens to sounds

▶ Interacts with others

▶ Anticipation and curiosity

Taking it further

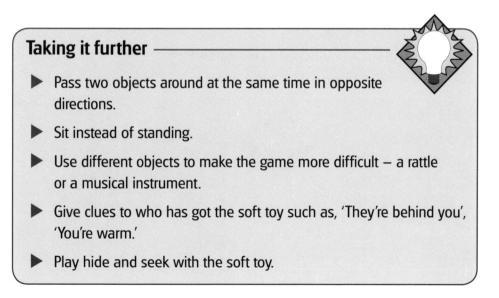

▶ Pass two objects around at the same time in opposite directions.

▶ Sit instead of standing.

▶ Use different objects to make the game more difficult – a rattle or a musical instrument.

▶ Give clues to who has got the soft toy such as, 'They're behind you', 'You're warm.'

▶ Play hide and seek with the soft toy.

Who Am I?

What you need:

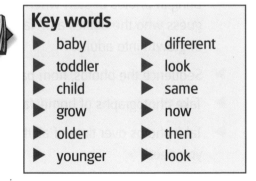

- a selection of photographs of the children at different stages – babies, toddlers and now
- mirrors

Key words
- baby
- toddler
- child
- grow
- older
- younger
- different
- look
- same
- now
- then
- look

What to do:

1. You could ask parents if they would lend or give you some baby photos if you haven't got them.

2. Sit with the children and talk about growth and development: babies – toddlers – child.

3. Look at the photos at each stage and talk about then and now, what we used to be like, be able to do.

4. Can the children recognise themselves as babies?

5. Use mirrors to look at themselves, including hair and eye colour, size, shape.

Look, listen and note:

▶ Recognition

▶ Sense of belonging

▶ Sequencing

▶ Interacts and works with others

Taking it further

▶ Ask parents for photos of themselves and make 'My Family Book'.

▶ Bring in photos of staff when they were children. Can the children guess who the babies are? Talk about now and then and the cycle of growth into adults.

▶ Sequence the photos, from babies to adults.

▶ Take photographs of home, family life, holidays.

▶ Take photos over time of all the children, so you have the resources you need.

Let's Paint

Focus
Attention skills through physical literacy

What you need:

▶ wallpaper

▶ sellotape

▶ paint in various colours

▶ a selection of different sized paint brushes

▶ four aprons

▶ large open space outside with a wall

I will need

Key words

▶ paint   ▶ colours

▶ draw   ▶ look

▶ lines   ▶ shades

▶ patterns   ▶ mix

▶ tracks   ▶ different

What to do:

1. Allow four children at a time for this activity.

2. Cover a large area on the wall with the wallpaper and secure it with sellotape.

3. Place a range of paint pots and brushes at the side of the area.

4. Stand back and observe the children being creative with the paint. When they have finished, stand back and talk about what they have done. Take some photos before you offer the activity to another group.

Look, listen and note:

▶ Enjoys own and others paintings.

▶ Sustains attentive listening

▶ Responds to instructions

▶ Fun and enjoyment

Taking it further

▶ Offer some additional resources – chalks, pens, glitter, collage, glue.

▶ Group together colours e.g. in autumn use orange, yellow and red paints.

▶ Take the activity inside and cover a table with wallpaper.

▶ Use the children's painting as backing paper for a display.

▶ Let the children mix their own paint.

Teddy's Adventure

Focus
Sustaining interest and attention

What you need:

- a teddy bear
- a rucksack
- large scrapbook
- disposable or children's camera
- pens and pencils

I will need

Key words

- journey
- photos
- new
- day
- excitement
- night
- home
- stay
- take turns
- visit
- look

What to do:

1. Introduce the teddy bear, give him a name and talk about how he likes going on trips and holidays with his rucksack and camera.

2. During the day include teddy in the daily routine, taking photographs of what teddy has done.

3. Let each child take it in turns to take teddy home.

4. Encourage families to take photos of teddy and for children to draw pictures and do mark making to tell stories of what and where teddy has been.

5. Record teddy's adventures in the scrapbook.

Look, listen and note:

▶ Sequencing events

▶ Listens to and responds

▶ Working together, sharing, taking turns

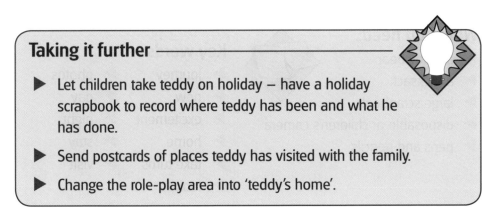

Taking it further

▶ Let children take teddy on holiday – have a holiday scrapbook to record where teddy has been and what he has done.

▶ Send postcards of places teddy has visited with the family.

▶ Change the role-play area into 'teddy's home'.

What's the Time Mr Wolf?

Focus
Anticipation

What you need:
- ▶ large area outside
- ▶ chalk

I will need

Key words
- ▶ steps
- ▶ time
- ▶ wait
- ▶ look
- ▶ ready
- ▶ dinner
- ▶ forwards
- ▶ quick
- ▶ run
- ▶ go
- ▶ home
- ▶ foot
- ▶ slow
- ▶ hungry

What to do:

1. Chalk two lines on the floor – one for Mr Wolf, one for the children's home.

2. Choose one child to be 'Mr Wolf'.

3. Stand Mr Wolf some distance away from the rest of the children and facing the other way.

4. The children ask, 'What's the time Mr Wolf?' Mr Wolf replies, 'One o'clock'.

5. Whatever time Mr Wolf replies, the children take that many steps forwards – towards Mr Wolf.

6. When Mr Wolf says 'It's dinner time!', the children must run back home before Mr Wolf catches them.

Look, listen and note:

▶ Waits with anticipation

▶ Working together, taking turns, copying and sharing

▶ Listens with enjoyment

▶ Explores and uses imagination

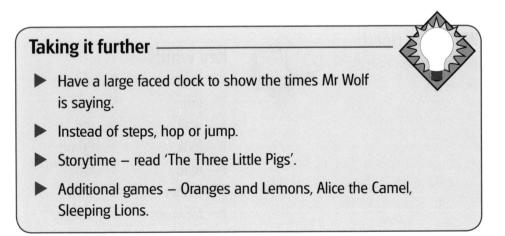

Taking it further

▶ Have a large faced clock to show the times Mr Wolf is saying.

▶ Instead of steps, hop or jump.

▶ Storytime – read 'The Three Little Pigs'.

▶ Additional games – Oranges and Lemons, Alice the Camel, Sleeping Lions.

The Builders' Yard

Focus
Concentration

What you need:

- a large outside area, building blocks and cones
- empty milk crates
- tools
- buckets, spades, rulers, tape measures, clipboards, pens, plans dressing up clothes – boots, jeans, toolkit belts and hard hats

Key words
- build
- hat
- tower
- tall
- fall
- crash
- walls
- tools
- measure
- patterns
- investigate
- sequence
- dig

What to do:

1. In a corner outside, create a builders' yard. Define the area using the empty milk crates.

2. Have four hard hats – only children wearing a hard hat are allowed in the builder's yard.

3. Discuss the items – What are they used for? How can we build/make...?

4. Discuss health and safety .

5. Observe the builders in the builders' yard - you may be surprised at what the children know.

Look, listen and note:

▶ Working together – sharing, taking turns, copying

▶ Listens to, understands and follow instructions

▶ Attention – how long did they stay engaged?

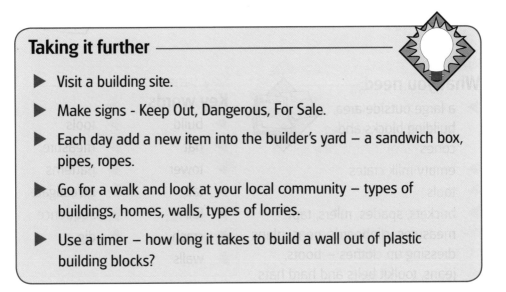

Taking it further

▶ Visit a building site.

▶ Make signs - Keep Out, Dangerous, For Sale.

▶ Each day add a new item into the builder's yard – a sandwich box, pipes, ropes.

▶ Go for a walk and look at your local community – types of buildings, homes, walls, types of lorries.

▶ Use a timer – how long it takes to build a wall out of plastic building blocks?

Watch it Grow

Focus
Sustained attention on the allotment

What you need:

- a suitable outside area – if struggling for space a large deep container or a grow bag will be fine
- top soil
- tools – forks, trowels
- a selection of plants, including broad beans and tomatoes
- suitable clothing

I will need

Key words

- soil
- seeds
- plant
- water
- sun
- protect
- look after
- grow
- cook
- eat
- dig
- weed
- trowel
- spade
- fork

What to do:

1. Let the children to help prepare the allotment ready to plant your plants.

2. Get dressed in suitable clothing. (You need suitable clothing too!)

3. Give all the children a tool and dig, plant, weed and water the plants.

4. Take some photos of the planting.

5. With the children do daily/weekly checks on the plants, care for them and monitor their growth through record charts and diaries.

6. Take photographs of the life cycle of the plants.

Look, listen and note:

▶ Explores and uses imagination

▶ Physical coordination

▶ Listens and responds to instructions

▶ Fun and enjoyment

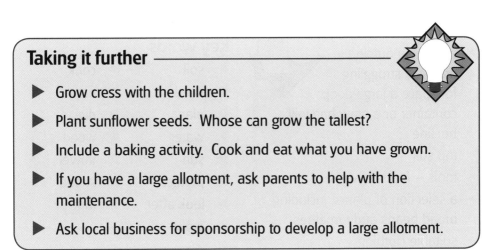

Taking it further

▶ Grow cress with the children.

▶ Plant sunflower seeds. Whose can grow the tallest?

▶ Include a baking activity. Cook and eat what you have grown.

▶ If you have a large allotment, ask parents to help with the maintenance.

▶ Ask local business for sponsorship to develop a large allotment.

Sounds of Fun

Focus
Listening skills

What you need:

- empty plastic bottles, rinsed well
- a quiet area
- water
- a measuring jug

I will need

Key words

- listen
- look
- pour
- measure
- sounds
- quiet
- loud
- same as
- blow
- shake
- whistle

What to do:

1. Using the measuring jug, measure out different quantities of water and pour into the bottles.

2. Stand the bottles next to each other in a line.

3. Carefully blow across the top of the bottles.

4. Listen to the sound each bottle makes. Can the children hear the difference?

5. Use different blowing techniques to create different sounds. Play your bottles in a band!

Look, listen and note:

▶ Listening to sounds

▶ Matching and sorting

▶ Sequencing

Taking it further

▶ Match two bottles together, do they make the same sound if they have the same level of water?

▶ Sequence the bottles from empty bottles to full bottles.

▶ Put stones in the bottles, secure the lid, shake the bottle and listen.

▶ Sing 'Ten Green Bottles'.

▶ Introduce food colouring and watch what happens to the water.

Sshh – What's That?

Focus
A listening walk

What you need:
- any environment

I will need

Key words
- listen
- hark
- hear
- loud
- quiet
- sshh
- what

What to do:

1. Take the children on a listening walk.

2. Whisper to them, 'We have to be quiet to hear the sounds'.

3. Creep round the environment listening to all the sounds.

4. When you hear a sound, stop, focus into that sound and talk softly about what's making that sound, what's it used for?

5. Carry on to the next noise.

6. Take some photos of the 'sound makers' so you can recreate your walk when you get back.

Look, listen and note:

▶ Listening and identifying sounds

▶ Listening, understanding and responding to instructions

▶ Working together

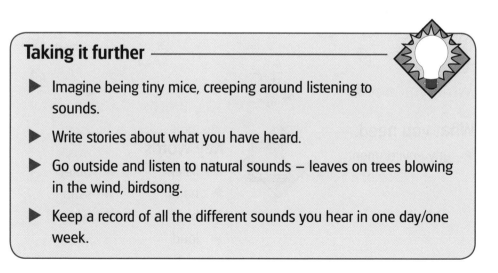

Taking it further

▶ Imagine being tiny mice, creeping around listening to sounds.

▶ Write stories about what you have heard.

▶ Go outside and listen to natural sounds – leaves on trees blowing in the wind, birdsong.

▶ Keep a record of all the different sounds you hear in one day/one week.

Mr Bear Likes Honey

Focus
Children's listening skills

What you need:
- a large area with minimum distractions
- a 'pot of honey' – a container, or a yellow bean bag

I will need

Key words
- bear
- honey
- listen
- quick
- note
- hear
- run
- what
- noise
- creep
- quiet
- tiptoe

What to do:

1. Sit with the children in a circle with the 'pot of honey' in the middle.

2. Choose a child to be Mr Bear who sleeps next to the honey.

3. While Mr Bear sleeps, choose another child to creep up and take the honey without waking Mr Bear whilst singing – 'Mr Bear likes honey buzz, buzz, buzz. I wonder why he does, does, does. Quick Mr Bear someone has your honey'.

4. When Mr Bear hears someone creeping up, he 'wakes up' and chases them round the circle back to their place.

5. The child who takes the honey is the next Mr Bear.

Look, listen and note:

▶ Working together – sharing, taking turns, copying and watching

▶ Listens to sounds

▶ Attention – how long did they stay engaged?

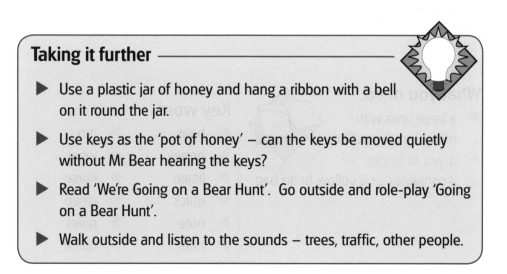

Taking it further

▶ Use a plastic jar of honey and hang a ribbon with a bell on it round the jar.

▶ Use keys as the 'pot of honey' – can the keys be moved quietly without Mr Bear hearing the keys?

▶ Read 'We're Going on a Bear Hunt'. Go outside and role-play 'Going on a Bear Hunt'.

▶ Walk outside and listen to the sounds – trees, traffic, other people.

Guess Who?

Focus
A listening game

What you need:
- a quiet undisturbed area
- a blindfold/mask – optional

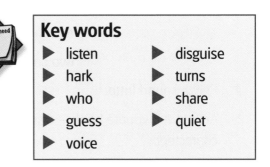

Key words
- listen
- hark
- who
- guess
- voice
- disguise
- turns
- share
- quiet

What to do:

1. Blindfold one child or turn the child away from the rest of the group and ask them to hide their face using their own hands.

2. All sing -   'Hello, hello, how are you today?

   Hello, hello, can you guess my name?'

3. One child says hello.

4. Can the blindfolded child identify who is saying hello?

5. Take turns in guessing and being blindfolded.

6. Some children hate blindfolds, be sensitive. Sometimes a flight mask from an airplane works better than fabric.

Look, listen and note:

▶ Listening to sounds

▶ Matching and sorting sounds

▶ Taking turns

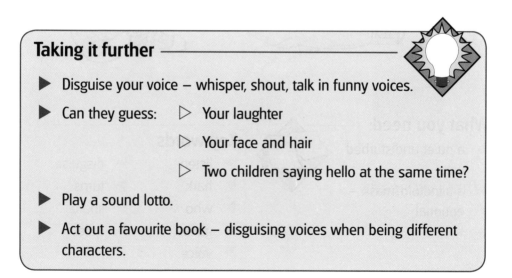

Taking it further

▶ Disguise your voice – whisper, shout, talk in funny voices.

▶ Can they guess: ▷ Your laughter

   ▷ Your face and hair

   ▷ Two children saying hello at the same time?

▶ Play a sound lotto.

▶ Act out a favourite book – disguising voices when being different characters.

Fancy Voices

Focus
A fun way to count

What you need:
- ▶ counting bricks
- ▶ imagination!

What to do:

1. Build a tower from one to ten, counting as you do so.

2. Now get the children to count the bricks using different voices – whispers, shouts, happy, angry, baby, fairy, etc.

3. Use your imagination to count in lots of funny and different voices.

Look, listen and note:

▶ Experimenting with sounds/voices

▶ Use of imagination and creativity

▶ Fun and enjoyment

Taking it further

▶ Have a set of animal face masks – can you count like a mouse, like a lion?

▶ Extend the counting to 15 then 20.

▶ Let the children decide how they are going to count.

▶ Use funny voices to tell stories, sing songs.

▶ Have a mirror so you can see yourself and what facial expressions you make.

A Shopping Trip

Focus

Listening and sequencing a story

What you need:

▶ comfy cushions
▶ a teddy bear

Key words

▶ shop	▶ what
▶ teddy bear	▶ how
▶ listen	▶ turn
▶ look	▶ buy
▶ next	▶ money

What to do:

1. Sit with the children and introduce the teddy. Tell them that Teddy has been shopping.

2. Hold the teddy and say, 'Today teddy went shopping and bought a hat'.

3. Pass the teddy to a child and repeat the story so far.

4. The child then adds something else that the teddy has bought.

5. Repeat until you have five items, then see if the children can remember what teddy has bought.

Look, listen and note:

▶ Listens with enjoyment to stories

▶ Retells stories

▶ Explores with imagination

Taking it further

▶ Change the story – teddy needs the hat to go to a wedding, to go to the park, it's raining or it's sunny. What does he see when he goes out? Add an object each time. Where does the story and shopping go now?

▶ Have a prop box of different things teddy could buy.

▶ Have some fun and make up funny stories or stories involving the children in the group.

▶ Actually take teddy to the shops!

Tell Me a Story

Focus

Use imagination and creativity to act out a story

What you need:

▶ 'The Enormous Turnip' Ladybird Tales book

▶ various dressing up clothes

▶ animal face masks

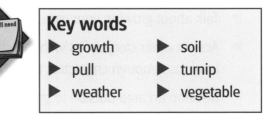

Key words

▶ growth   ▶ soil

▶ pull   ▶ turnip

▶ weather   ▶ vegetable

What to do:

1. Read the story with the children.

2. Talk to the children about the story and how turnips grow.

3. Show the children the various dressing up clothes and animal face masks and help them to decide which character they want to be. Ensure there are enough props for all the children to participate.

4. Read the story again for the children while they act out 'The Enormous Turnip', adding characters to the story as needed.

Look, listen and note:

▶ Listens with enjoyment to stories

▶ Retells stories

▶ Explores with imagination

▶ Working together – sharing, taking turns, watching

Taking it further

▶ Follow on the story with the children by drawing their character.

▶ Collate all the characters and make the children's own 'Enormous Turnip' book.

▶ Take and print photos of the story session and use these for further activities, including a sequence of the story.

▶ Talk about growing your own vegetables, why and how.

▶ Act out other storybooks with the children. Ensure your chosen book has enough characters to allow all the children to participate.

▶ Develop an area outside to grow your own vegetables. Broad beans are easy vegetables to grow.

Look!

Focus
Investigate and explore light and pattern

What you need:

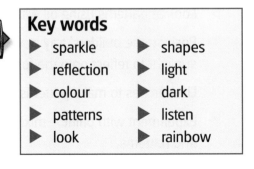

- a selection of coloured transparent paddles, prisms, bubble makers, kaleidoscopes, crystals, CDs and mirrors
- kitchen foil
- a large builders' tray

Key words
- sparkle
- reflection
- colour
- patterns
- look
- shapes
- light
- dark
- listen
- rainbow

What to do:

1. Cover the builders' tray with the foil.

2. Place the selection of objects onto the tray.

3. Sit with the children and show them the objects and how they work.

4. Encourage the children to explore and investigate, looking specifically at colours, shapes, patterns, reflections and light.

5. Allow plenty of time for the children to experiment with the objects.

Look, listen and note:

▶ Explore and investigation

▶ Shows curiosity

▶ Working together

Taking it further

▶ Make a den and explore shiny materials in the dark.

▶ Look at patterns using oil with water in containers.

▶ Position the builders' tray next to a window/door and use the sunlight to reflect onto the foil.

▶ Use torches to make patterns and reflections.

▶ Experiment with paint – mixing colours together, looking at shades and patterns.

Book List

'The Tiny Seed' Classic Board book by Eric Carle
(Little Simon, 2005) ISBN: 9780689871498

'Jasper's Beanstalk' (Hardcover) by Nick Butterworth and Mick Inkpen
(Hodder Children's Books, 1992) ISBN 9780340556603

The Little Book of Dance by Julie Quinn and Naomei Wager
(A&C Black, 2009) ISBN 9781904187745

'The Jolly Polly Postman' by Allan Ahlberg and Janet Ahlberg
(LB Kids, 2006) ISBN 9780316017763

'The Enormous Turnip' Ladybird First Favourite Tales book
(Ladybird, 1999) ISBN 9780721497389

The Little Books Club

There is always something in Little Books to help and inspire you. Packed full of lovely ideas, Little Books meet the need for exciting and practical activities that are fun to do, address the Early Learning Goals and can be followed in most settings. Everyone is a winner!

We publish 5 new Little Books a year. Little Books Club members receive each of these 5 books as soon as they are published for a reduced price. The subscription cost is £37.50 – a one off payment that buys the 5 new books for £7.50 instead of £8.99 each.

In addition to this, Little Books Club Members receive:
· Free postage and packing on anything ordered from the Featherstone catalogue
· A 15% discount voucher upon joining which can be used to buy any number of books from the Featherstone catalogue
· Members price of £7.50 on any additional Little Book purchased
· A regular, free newsletter dealing with club news, special offers and aspects of Early Years curriculum and practice
· All new Little Books on approval - return in good condition within 30 days and we'll refund the cost to your club account

Call 020 7440 2446 or email: littlebooks@acblack.com for an enrolment pack. Or download an application form from our website:
www.acblack.com/featherstone

The **Little Books** series consists of:

All Through the Year

Bags, Boxes & Trays

Bricks and Boxes

Celebrations

Christmas

Circle Time

Clay and Malleable
Materials

Clothes and Fabrics

Colour, Shape and Number

Cooking from Stories

Cooking Together

Counting

Dance

Dance, with music CD

Discovery Bottles

Dough

50

Fine Motor Skills

Fun on a Shoestring

Games with Sounds

Growing Things

ICT

Investigations

Junk Music

Language Fun

Light and Shadow

Listening

Living Things

Look and Listen

Making Books and Cards

Making Poetry

Mark Making

Maths Activities

Maths from Stories

Maths Songs and Games

Messy Play

Music

Nursery Rhymes

Outdoor Play

Outside in All Weathers

Parachute Play

Persona Dolls

Phonics

Playground Games

Prop Boxes for Role Play

Props for Writing

Puppet Making

Puppets in Stories

Resistant Materials

Role Play

Sand and Water

Science through Art

Scissor Skills

Sewing and Weaving

Small World Play

Sound Ideas

Storyboards

Storytelling

Seasons

Time and Money

Time and Place

Treasure Baskets

Treasureboxes

Tuff Spot Activities

Washing Lines

Writing

All available from

www.acblack.com/featherstone